P9-CRV-920

SPIRITUAL RESILIENCE

SPIRITUAL RESILIENCE
30 Days to Refresh Your Soul

Robert J. Wicks

Franciscan
MEDIA
Cincinnati, Ohio

Portions of this book were originally published in a different format under the title *Seeking Perspective*, ISBN 978-0-80913-234-8.

Scripture quotations are from *The Revised Standard Version of the Bible: Catholic Edition*, copyright © 1965, 1966 the Division of Christian Education of the National Council of the Churches of Christ in the United States of America. Used by permission. All rights reserved.

Cover design by LUCAS Art & Design, Jenison, Michigan
Cover image © Masterfile
Book design by Mark Sullivan

LIBRARY OF CONGRESS CATALOGING-IN-PUBLICATION DATA
Wicks, Robert J.
Spiritual resilience : 30 days to refresh your soul / Robert J. Wicks.
pages cm
Includes bibliographical references.
ISBN 978-1-61636-886-9 (alk. paper)
1. Resilience (Personality trait)—Religious aspects—Christianity—Miscellanea.
2. Crisis management—Religious aspects—Christianity—Miscellanea. I. Title.
BV4597.58.R47W53 2015
248.8'6—dc23
2014038012

ISBN 978-1-61636-886-9
Copyright ©2015, Robert J. Wicks. All rights reserved.

Published by Franciscan Media
28 W. Liberty St.
Cincinnati, OH 45202
www.FranciscanMedia.org
Printed in the United States of America.
Printed on acid-free paper.
15 16 17 18 19 5 4 3 2 1

RELATED BOOKS BY ROBERT J. WICKS

Perspective: The Calm Within the Storm
(Oxford University Press, 2014)

Bounce: Living the Resilient Life
(Oxford University Press, 2010)

*Riding the Dragon: 10 Lessons on Inner Strength
in Challenging Times*
(Sorin Books, 2003/2012)

In memory of loved ones who made a real difference
in the lives of those who knew them…

RON & NOEL WICKS

DOT BEGLANE

LARRY LANZA

MICHAELE QUEVEDO

CONTENTS

FOREWORD

Some pundit suggested that there is a ninth beatitude: "Blessed are the flexible, for they will not get bent out of shape." Resilience is the name of the game. The human journey is messy, perilous, and challenging. At times we are stretched beyond our limit, bent over by incredible burdens, compressed by worries and anxieties. The resilient ones have the ability to recover from life's "slings and arrows"; the resilient ones have the capacity to adjust to the misfortunes and stresses of life.

Dr. Copeland, in Carson McCullers's *The Heart is a Lonely Hunter*, offers words of wisdom in stating that "the most fatal thing" a person can do is attempt to go through life alone. That same message runs through these thirty reflections on striving for spiritual resilience. We need one another to sustain perspective, to experience the mystery of God's love, to cope with the peaks and valleys of life. There is in this volume an integration of psychology and spirituality from an author who has been in the trenches as well as being a widely read scholar and prolific author. Drawing from a plethora of authors—Karl Rahner, Martin Luther, Henri Nouwen, Basil Pennington, Thomas Merton, John Wesley, Abraham Heschel, Pierre Teilhard de Chardin, William Sloane Coffin, and many others—Robert J. Wicks provides both insights and practical suggestions on how to grow emotionally and spiritually by confronting courageously and wisely the ups and downs of life. This is not a book to be read in the course of a few hours. Rather, it is a text that calls for meditation and interaction, a journal, if you will, on patterns of human growth.

The focus in *Spiritual Resilience* is clear: care and compassion for all of us who, at one time or another, will experience sickness, sadness, loneliness, stress, and loss. No exemptions here; everyone needs some insight and inspiration, practical guidance, and encouragement. In times of crisis there are paradigms and actions that can help navigate the rapids of life's river. Not only is human counsel helpful (and, at times, necessary), but one's faith life is supremely important. Dr. Wicks argues that "spirituality can inform and support good psychology rather than the other way round." Thus the stress on silence and solitude, on experiencing God's extravagant love and mercy, on embracing the covenant that God offers us.

This volume is realistic. It probes our confusions and anxieties, our negativities and passivities, our moments of embarrassment and awkwardness. It's all about mental health and spiritual wisdom.

What comes to mind with the word *resilience* is the ability to bounce back. When we have God's covenant in our life, when we have solidarity with others, when our expectations are realistic, and when we maintain perspective, we will not only be healthy, we will be agents of light, love, and life for others.

The book's subtitle—*30 Days to Refresh Your Soul*—captures well one of the greatest needs of our time! Too easily our lives narrow down to a specific difficulty or trauma that then becomes absolutized, a part that becomes the whole. Robert Wicks performs a great service in helping us to keep a healthy perspective and offers practical steps on how to do that. By staying flexible, hopefully we will not be bent out of shape; by staying resilient, we will come to know that peace and joy, as St. Paul says, surpasses all understanding.

Bishop Robert F. Morneau
Auxiliary Bishop Emeritus of Green Bay
Pastor of Resurrection Parish

INTRODUCTION

Be Clear and Be Not Afraid

Spiritual resilience is not simply about recovering from adversity. It is about bouncing back in a way that deeper knowledge of both God and self may result. With the right guidance, during difficult times and periods of confusion, pain, and stress, we have a unique opportunity to nurture our relationship with God and enable it to grow in surprising ways.

Given this powerful possibility, over the next thirty days, we will be guided by key spiritual figures as well as wisdom that I have been able to glean from my own relevant experiences to help others nurture the simple care of a hopeful heart. To accomplish this, the reflections that follow seek to offer insight, practical information, and inspiration during periods of sickness, sadness, loneliness, stress, and loss. Anxiety and uncertainty in the world today may not be any greater than it has been in the past, but if we're caught up in it at the moment, these thoughts may open us to see clearly, act faithfully, and appreciate more deeply that we are loved by God—no matter how dark or puzzling things seem at certain times in our own lives and in the world.

One of the difficulties we may have when our lives become unmanageable is that we find dealing with other people to be difficult and we may even struggle to maintain a relationship with God. Caring people especially can find themselves carrying unnecessary crosses as they become lost in the maze of trying to meet everyone's crazy expectations—including their own!

The central tenet of this book is: "Be clear and be not afraid, for you are loved by God." And it is in this spirit that I offer this work to you. In keeping with this, I have tried to offer some useful themes and practical approaches to deal with certain psychological and spiritual difficulties and challenges. To accomplish this, I have selected thirty points that may lead to the kind of spiritual resilience that encourages us to be more responsive to God and be closer in solidarity with others. In doing this, we have the opportunity to become more alive, possibly in ways we could never have imagined.

An organized way to reflect on the material presented for each day is to use the following steps:

In the morning before beginning the day's activities, read the phrase at the beginning of that day's entry and spend some time reflecting on it.

Recall it several times during the day and see how it is applicable to the activities, feelings, thoughts, and images you are having today.

In the evening, in a spirit of thankfulness to God, recall this same theme just before going to bed. This is also an ideal time to jot down any reflections you might have with respect to it. (This is optional of course. If it becomes more of a chore than it is worth, omit doing it.)

The nice thing about following this approach is that although the process will take only a few minutes each day, many of the basic themes and insights, as well as related thoughts that emerge in your own mind, will have an opportunity to take root and bear new fruit. You may find that some of the points may not have any meaning for you at the time. Others may be of only short-term value. Some, I hope, will prove of lasting value. By approaching the material in this way, you will have given the overall theme of spiritual resilience a higher profile in your outlook on life. You may be surprised by the results.

The final step, after having finished a month of scattered minutes of reflection, is to take a few more moments to see what overall paradigm you have come up with in how you wish to lead a life marked by greater spiritual resilience. In other words, what one or two sentences seem to sum up the lessons of inner strength, perspective, and clarity you learned? What one phrase might easily help you to recall the presence of God in your life and quickly bring to mind a healthy attitude in how you approach life—especially in difficult or confusing circumstances?

For me, psychological clarity is possible and desirable because the truth sets me free from the bondage of illusion, and I believe the truth is only really approachable when I feel deeply loved by God. The phrases and ideas I have chosen here reflect that core belief. However, each of us is different, so the phrase you will find powerful for you may be different than mine. As you go through each day's reflection, you might want to formulate your own theme of perspective. The phrase should be broad enough to reflect an overall approach to meeting life but specific enough to be of use.

PART ONE

SPIRITUAL STRENGTH
A Psychological Resource During Difficult Times

"A domesticated deity does not call us out to the spiritual pilgrimage. He legitimates where we already are."[1]

—URBAN HOLMES

Much has been written on the integration of psychology and spirituality. Still more has been written on how psychology can aid in the development of a mature faith. However, with the exception of Gerald May and several others, not enough has been written on how spirituality can inform and support good psychology rather than the other way round. Yet this is exactly what I am referring to when I talk about spiritual strength as a psychological resource during difficult times.

To begin, I would like to focus on the role that faith, prayer, and spirituality can play as psychological resources in times of crisis and loss. A crisis can cause stress on self-esteem and encourage a distorted sense of self-awareness. A strong and grounded spirituality can work to counter that stress. Faith can be a force with which to fight despair and cynicism. Faith can transform doubt into something positive—a new opening to a greater sense of God and life.

DAY 1

> Spirituality dawns when God becomes as real as the problems
> and joys we face each day.

During the very times when losses occur and crises strike, the opportunity is especially present for us to realize how much God is at the center of our lives, at the heart of ourselves, and on the horizon of our destiny in new, refreshing ways. Until then, the covenant we have with God may be vague, a mere backdrop, or practically forgotten. It isn't the deep relationship implied by the word *covenant*. A crisis or loss can shake the dust of denial off of our possibly childish relationship with the Lord; it can remind us of our vulnerability and dependence on the creator and cut through the massive games of pseudo-independence we have played. Our first response to this shaking may well be to cry out in anguish, shock, anxiety, impatience, and indignation at our tragedy.

When serious problems arise, patience and a respectful, distant pleading with God don't last long. Perhaps you've heard the expression "as patient as Job." A cursory examination of the text reveals that he spent six chapters in patient acceptance and thirty-six chapters complaining and lamenting. In most instances we are just like him in this regard. When God doesn't answer us as we would like, when the status quo is not returned to its original luster, we may feel unfairly tested and be furious or feel let down. We may doubt God's presence in our lives. At times such as these, we can also become angry about what we perceive as the hide-and-seek game we believe God is playing with us at the very time when we feel a dramatic need for that divine presence. As a matter of fact, if we are really being honest with ourselves, at times like these, we may question whether a God exists at all.

Henri Nouwen recognizes this tendency toward doubt about God when facing a crisis and the role "secularization" plays in it. He notes:

> It is very simplistic to say that emergencies make people pay more attention to God and reawaken religious feelings. We might in fact wonder if the opposite is not more often the case.
>
> Fear and anger do not lead to God. The great pressures of our time have created much bitterness, resentment, and hatred.
>
> Many people have turned away from God and prayer since they no longer see how they can pray to a God who allows so much cruelty, so much agony, so much pain…. We listen to lectures affirming the importance of prayer, but we really think that our people need actions and not prayer and that prayer and praying is good when you really have nothing else to do. I wonder if under the surface of our religiosity we do not have great doubts about God's effectiveness in our world, about his interest in us—yes, even about his presence among us. I wonder if many of us are not plagued by deep, hostile feelings toward God and the idea of God without having any way to express them. I even wonder if there are many religious people for whom God is their only concern…. When we speak of our age as a secular age, we must first of all be willing to become aware of how deeply this secularism has entered into our own

hearts and how doubt, hesitation, suspicion, anger, and even hatred corrode our relationship with God.[2]

When a serious crisis arises, we outwardly—or at least inwardly—argue, bargain, express our feelings of abandonment, and become angry or hurt that God is allowing this to happen. We believe this to be "malevolent neglect." In response, it is no wonder that we become noisy. Now this style of relating to God and God's messages to us is actually not really bad. As a matter of fact, grappling with God and the words of revelation has a long respected religious tradition, particularly in Judaism.

Rabbi Lionel Blue, a past Convenor of the Religious Court of the Reform Synagogues of Great Britain, reminds us:

> Judaism is a noisy religion. The faithful are rarely silent.... Jews even study the divine law traditionally in pairs, so that they can argue better...the meaning of the name Israel [is] "one who struggles with God." It was not given to Jacob after quiet meditation, but after [a] prolonged and realistic struggle with a messenger of God.... [Jews] are not holy vegetables, bits of religious asparagus, [just] quietly growing upwards, complying with divine requirements, in a dull earthly silence.[3]

In taking the covenant seriously, Jews are quite actively involved with God. This should be true of the committed followers of any monotheistic religion who encounter "the Other" as someone real, someone true, someone meaningful in their daily lives.

Expressing anguish, disillusionment and near despair with a deeply felt desire for a return of what we have lost or a return to a pre-crisis state is natural. I feel, as many others do, that expressing initial strong negative reactions to God during difficult times is not a problem in itself. As a matter of fact, it may be one of the signs of a faith that is real and based on an ongoing relationship with the living God.

The difficulty arises when we don't move beyond anger and disillusionment with God in order to be open to the possibilities of encountering God in surprising and mysterious ways. The greatest challenge in times of crisis and loss is to be willing to be open to receive love in new ways, possibly from different sources at unexpected times.

Seeking Greater Spiritual Resilience and a Healthier Perspective...

- How does your relationship with God mirror other relationships in your life?
- How reluctant are you to admit that you're angry with God?
- When have you felt God's presence in the midst of a terrible crisis?

DAY 2

"It is not your duty to finish the work, but you are not free to neglect it."

—RABBI TARPHON

Even when we know we are loved deeply by God, we will still fight hard and furiously against injustice, sickness, poverty, death, and loss. In doing this, at times, we may lament loudly and directly to God, asking that a burden be lifted from our shoulders. But, at the same time, we must also begin to know more deeply that we can never return to the "fleshpots" of Egypt, or remove the necessary crosses that come with being where God wants us to be.

Difficult periods in our lives are special times to remember. Remember what? Remember the covenant. Remember the availability of God's grace. And remember that no matter what befalls us, God will not abandon us. Aware of our close relationship with the Ultimate in this way, we will look desperately for God in the situation—not God as we would have the creator appear, but the God who in mysterious ways can be like a burning bush that consumes and purifies our doubts. The God we seek supports our spirit and calls us to stand dependent and barefoot on holy ground. There we can meet true Wisdom so she can embrace us and urge us to open our eyes even though we may prefer to keep them shut.

A contemporary of Jesus, Rabbi Tarphon said: "The day is short, the work is great, the laborers are sluggish, the wages are high, and the Master of the house is insistent. It is not your duty to finish the work, but you are not free to neglect it."[4] In the Gospels, this theme is expressed as "the road to Jerusalem." Just as Jesus resolutely traveled to Jerusalem, knowing that crucifixion awaited him, we know that we need to seek God's will and embrace God's support in all situations—even the necessarily painful ones.

Sometimes we believe that religion will protect us from losing what we love and have in life. Such religion gets distorted and can actually block us from experiencing the actual *living* God. We mistake our image of God and the gifts of God for the true, undefinable God. Abraham Heschel, who comes from a long line of Hasidic rabbis, makes this point quite poetically:

> As a tree torn from the soil, as a river separated from its source, the human soul wanes when detached from what is greater than itself…. It is the attachment to what is spiritually superior: loyalty to a sacred person or idea, devotion to a noble friend or teacher, love for a people or for mankind, which holds our inner life together. But any ideal, human, social, or artistic, if it forms a roof over all of life, shuts us off from the light. Even the palm of one hand may bar the light of the entire sun. Indeed, we must be open to the remote in order to perceive the near. Unless we aspire to the utmost, we shrink to inferiority.[5]

And so, within the tragedy of a loss or crisis there is a real possibility to move away from the limited God we have created, and a life we may be merely existing within, to an experience of God and life that can be real and transforming in nature. Still, admitting this and believing it at such a deep level that one can boldly act upon it are two completely different things! A life of true covenant is simple...but not easy.

Seeking Greater Spiritual Resilience and a Healthier Persective...

- How do you reconcile an all-loving God with the tragedy and suffering that seem so pervasive in our lives and our world?

DAY 3

"People live cautiously because they pray cautiously."
—James Fenhagen

The problems we have on a social as well as on an individual scale can be very great, and it is easy to be overwhelmed by them. We pollute the waters, sky, land, and our foods. We are faced with hunger, violence, terrorism, and the fear of incurable disease. We have been given a beautiful, untamed world and we have frequently responded by destroying much of it in an ill-fated attempt to conquer its possibilities. Too infrequently do we sit with our gifts from God and affiliate with the world in a way in which the plants that grow, the fish that swim the seas, and the animals that populate the earth can flourish with us.

Unfortunately for us, God frequently seems so absent, so unreal in these troubled days. If we are authentic in times as these, we may ask ourselves and our religion again and again: "What possibilities can faith and spirituality really offer us as resources during a time of crisis?"

This is where true prayer and a deep, thoroughly challenging sense of spirituality come in and are given the opportunity to surprise us, move us to a new level of personal integration, help us become more spiritually resilient, and of course, lead to essential social action. One of my favorite quotes with respect to this reality is from Jim Fenhagen, who was the dean of General Theological Seminary in New York and the author of *Invitation to Holiness*. He writes: "People live cautiously because they pray cautiously."[6]

In a time of crisis or loss, when our lament for a return of the status quo fails, a natural inclination is to be conservative and hesitant in our belief because the results we want, in the way we want them when we want them, don't seem very visible. As a result, it may not seem sensible to continue to believe. However, we must try *not* to be sensible, as the world might have us be in this regard, because at times like these, true prayer throws caution to the wind and lets us be open in a way that our faith and spirituality can form a new basis for psychological awareness and growth. And this is exactly what we need to happen—especially during difficult times!

Seeking Greater Spiritual Resilience and a Healthier Perspective…

- What can prayer change in the midst of a crisis? If it's not a magic wand, then what is it?
- People sometimes criticize a reliance on prayer and religion as being useless and even harmful. How does your experience of prayer compare to this attitude?

DAY 4

"We must be faithful in little things in order to be permitted to hope that God in his grace will also send us faithfulness in great things."

—KARL RAHNER

Without faith and the deep sense of covenant that comes with it, a loss can often set the stage for cynicism and a despairing sense of doubt that digs a deep hole from which one's human enthusiasm may never be able to fully emerge again. This is especially so in the case of the young. As Maya Angelou, poet and author of the stirring autobiography *I Know Why the Caged Bird Sings*, aptly notes: "There is nothing so tragic as a young cynic. For the young cynic is going from knowing nothing to believing nothing."[7]

People of faith, the spiritually committed, can often feel the love of God and their own love for God lying just below the surface of their psyches. They live their lives with a preconscious awareness of God's incarnational love, and it is reinforced on a daily basis by an almost prelogical form of communication with the presence of God in the world. This daily contact with God is necessary to set the stage for those dramatic periods in our lives that will lift up and befall all of us at certain times in life.

The theologian Karl Rahner addresses this theme in the following way:

> We cannot assert that someone who is well behaved, devout, and virtuous in ordinary life, is also already certain of surviving the great situations where it is a question of life or death. The grace of such endurance is a grace that no one can merit by good behavior in ordinary life. But ordinary life is indeed the way in which we must remain ready for the decisive situations; it can be the way in which God wants to give us the very grace—which we cannot demand—of surviving the great hours of our life. We must be faithful in little things in order to be permitted to hope that God in his grace will also send us faithfulness in great things.[8]

For Rahner, the grace of God upholds us during difficult times. That grace isn't something that we build up by years of prayer and devotions. But those small and daily acts of faith can give us a foundation.

Seeking Greater Spiritual Resilience and a Healthier Perspective...
- What are some of your regular prayer routines? How faithful are you to those routines?
- What might you do to make prayer a more regular part of your life—in good times as well as bad?

DAY 5

"The pious [person] needs no miraculous communication to make him [or her] aware of God's presence."

—Abraham Heschel

Yesterday we looked at the way daily contact with God can increase our spiritual resilience and make us more prepared for the difficult times and dramatic events that are part of all of our lives.

Rabbi Heschel takes a slightly different approach than theologian Karl Rahner that is worthy of note here as well. For him, the person of prayer is aware at all times of the closeness of God:

Whatever the pious [person] does is linked to the divine; each smallest trifle is tangential to [God's] course. In breathing he uses [God's] force; in thinking he wields [God's] power. He moves always under the unseen canopy of remembrance, and the wonderful weight of the name of God rests steadily on his mind. The word of God is as vital to him as air or food. He is never alone, never companionless, for God is within reach of his heart.… The pious [person] needs no miraculous communication to make him aware of God's presence.… His awareness may be overlaid momentarily or concealed by some violent shift in consciousness, but it never fades away.[9]

In other words, persons of faith, at some level, are ready for crises, in the same way that they are ready for all daily occurrences, to open up new doors.

Seeking Greater Spiritual Resilience and a Healthier Perspective...
• What reminds you on a daily basis of God's providence?

DAY 6

> The amount of real trust we have in God is sometimes best measured by the depth of the doubt and the seriousness of the questions with which we are willing to live.

Although a crisis is just as painful for the spiritual person as it is for one who has little or no conscious faith, in the faithful individual the doubt does not point only to despair but—amidst the pain—to new hopes built on a renewed faith and a new dynamic image of God. As a matter of fact, as was noted above, the amount of real trust we have in God is sometimes best measured by the depth of the doubt and the seriousness of the questions with which we are willing to live.

Rather than removing the doubts, prayer may instead help us more and more to see the truth and hold onto the possible as well as the probable without pain. Serious believers are critical thinkers. When a crisis dawns and threatens the very core of their identity and their faith, they are willing to continue to respond and search—not because of religion (which in many cases loses its way because of an obsession over trivialities), but because of their belief in the living God and a desire to live with that God now in some new way, rather than to merely exist. (In psychology, this would be referred to as an openness to new meaning-making.)

Let me illustrate by relating an interaction with a person who was plunged into an unforeseen tragic crisis:

A woman and her fifty-year-old husband received word that he had been promoted to a key position in the Fortune 500 company in which he was employed. They were thrilled and prepared to move with their children to California. The move was coming any day and their garage was filled with boxes of household goods they had already packed.

Only days before they were due to leave, their daughter had a major argument with her father. Shortly after she had stormed out, he started to feel chest pain. He was rushed to the emergency room of a nearby hospital, but it was too late. He had such a massive coronary that nothing could be done to save him.

When the woman came to see me the next day, she was depressed and angry. She looked at me directly and said, "I want you to know how angry I am at God!" I sensed from her tone, the look on her face, and the fact that she knew my work was based on religion as well as psychology, that she expected me to defend God. When I replied that if I were in her position I would not be angry with God, she seemed ready to give me a real fight about it until I added, "Anger wouldn't be a strong enough word to describe how I would feel. I would be violently furious at God if what happened to you had happened to me!"

She then felt secure enough to share her wrath that this should happen to her. I helped her with this by encouraging her anger, and she let it out until, with a tired and somewhat dejected expression on her face, she mumbled that she appreciated my listening to her and got up to leave.

I stood up with her and said, "Before you go, I do want to tell you two things. First, you won't always feel as badly as you do right now. Do you believe that?" She replied, "No, I don't." I then said to her, "That's just as I expected. If you believed this so soon after your husband's death it would be unnatural. However, what I am saying is true. I have never lied to you so I won't lie to you now. As a result, even though you don't believe it in your heart and have yet to experience it when you feel really sad, I want you to remember my words, to hold onto them with all your might."

"Second, I hope that you don't stay angry at God any longer than you have to." At this comment, she came to life again and jutted her jaw out at me. She gave me a look that seemed to say, "I knew all along that you were going to defend God and tell me that I should not be angry with him." With this expression on her face, she challenged me in a harsh, raspy voice that spoke of sadness and anger, "Just give me one reason why you hope I won't stay angry at God after what's just happened to me!"

I replied: "Because when we are angry with someone we put up a wall between us and this person. And so we deprive ourselves of that person's love. Included in this love—which is probably the warmest love you can ever receive—is the love of God. I'm your friend. I know you need love during this really tough time; after all you have been through, I even feel you *deserve* it. So, I hope when the time is right, you can let the wall come down and let God love you."

Upon hearing this, she looked down, cried softly, hugged and thanked me, and left. It was far from easy, but eventually she did recover from this loss and is led an active, happy life.

Seeking Greater Spiritual Resilience and a Healthier Perspective...
• Who helps you hold on to your faith in times of doubt?

DAY 7

> By wrapping ourselves in silence, solitude, and gratitude, we can open our hearts in contemplation again and again to a healthier perspective and a greater sense of simplicity that will help us be more spiritually resilient.

When something terrible happens, it awakens us to life and the reality of our present limits and eventual death in a way that success, comfort, and prosperity never could. True prayer can serve as a counterbalance in such instances to the insulating and denying forces of a world that constantly encourages us to think otherwise or, more accurately, not to think clearly at all! Spiritual people ultimately have the opportunity to meet tragedy in a different way because they meet life in general in a different way. In prayer, by wrapping themselves in silence, solitude, and gratitude, they open their hearts in a contemplative way again and again to a new, healthier sense of perspective and a greater appreciation of true simplicity. They are able to hear God in a world of sorrows, joys, uncertainties, and limits because the lost art of listening, *really* listening, to the universe, can be gracefully recovered again and again in the sabbath experience of silence and solitude.

What I am speaking about here is not pietistical passivity. I am speaking about the willingness to accept life unconditionally and to fathom its possibilities within the limits of failure, sinfulness, and death.

Seeking Greater Spiritual Resilience and a Healthier Perspective…

- If you are someone who is uncomfortable with silence and solitude, how might you grow in appreciation of this type of prayer?

DAY 8

As resignation moves toward acceptance, real healing and crisis resolution take place.

A practical theme of the psychiatrist William Glasser, who was the author of books on *Reality Therapy* and *Choice Theory*, was that in life we must learn to recognize the givens, understand the givens, accept the givens and live within those very givens.[10] Faith, prayer, and spirituality can determine in a significant way how well we will do this. As resignation moves toward acceptance, real healing and crisis resolution takes place. A strong faith provides the inner environment where this can more readily occur and leads to greater integration and maturity—no matter what the problem.

A case in point is the way persons who have been diagnosed with a terminal illness lead their lives. After moving through all of the initial stages one naturally goes through after hearing the diagnosis, there is a crossroads. One path leads to denial and despair…the other to holiness. Spiritually attuned persons are in a good position to be firmly covenantal at such a crisis point. They have the possibility to be truly awake to a more meaningful relationship with self, others, and God than ever before; moreover, this enlightenment can pervade the rest of their lives. This does not mean that these persons would not still wish that a cure could be found in time to save them; also, periodic negativity in the form of depression, anxiety and anger might still stir within them, for this is natural and human—we must remember that holiness does not mean that we don't mourn losses or unwanted change. However, if their faith is strong, they are in a special position to experience life more deeply and richly than many of us who are "doomed" to live a long life of compulsive existence.

Now, let me present a contrast to illustrate my point. Most of my clinical practice is conducted with therapists and other professionals in the healing and helping areas. Once, a psychologist whose life was out of control consulted me. He reminded me of a person completely lost in the center of the city, desperately trying to find a route to his home in the suburbs but terribly stymied because he had a blindfold over his eyes. My intervention with him was metaphorically akin to telling him how to take the blindfold off so he could formulate a plan to free himself from his addiction to achieving "success" as he had envisioned it up to this point. Yet, instead of responding affirmatively to my suggestion his initial response to me essentially was: "I don't have the time to take off my blindfold; can't you see I'm too busy trying to find my way home?"

A healthy perspective, which is a key element in spiritual resilience, must be fought for each day if we are to maintain an awareness of what's really important without having to be awakened again and again by a crisis or loss. The choice is up to us, and a strong faith and spirituality that allows a quiet period each day to cut through the compulsive lies of life and helps us to breathe in the truth of knowing what really matters certainly can help in this regard.

Seeking Greater Spiritual Resilience and a Healthier Perspective…
- We all have a sense that we have issues we have not fully examined. Set aside some time today to reflect on one of those issues in your own life.

DAY 9

> Spiritual and psychological growth occurs only when insight
> encourages both our hearts and our minds to give up the
> "advantage" of staying the same in order to opt for something
> greater yet unknown.

After a time of crisis or loss has passed, we reach a point where we need to begin once again to move forward. It might be helpful at this point in our month's exercise to explore a contemplative style of prayer that can help us in such transitional times—and other times as well.

Spiritual and psychological growth occurs only when insight encourages both our hearts and our minds to give up the "advantage" of staying the same in order to opt for something that is greater, yet to this point, unknown. Prayer can be a great help in encouraging us to do this and strengthening us on the way.

Many of us have learned a style of centering prayer. If we haven't or if we've forgotten, the following steps can serve as a quick refresher:

Find a quiet place to sit and relax.

Put yourself in the presence of a loving God and wrap yourself in gratitude. If you don't have these feelings, pray for them as you continue.

Take either a centering word (Jesus), or read a few passages from the Bible or a spiritual book.

Sit with the spirit of what you have read or quietly repeat the centering word over and over again. If you become aware of anything else or are distracted, just let the issue move through your mind and out. If it persists, then hand it over to God rather than preoccupying yourself with it, which, after all, serves no purpose.

Sit quietly like this with the Lord in love for ten or twenty minutes a day on a regular basis, and your relationship with God will grow.

Seeking Greater Spiritual Resilience and a Healthier Perspective...

- Spend your prayer time today in centering prayer, letting go of the things with which you have been struggling. Acknowledge that God is in control of your life.

DAY 10

One of the greatest human paradoxes is that we seem to complain the most about a lack of spiritual passion in our lives at the very time when we are willing to gamble the least.

It is hard to have vision if we are busy holding on tightly to the present, are preoccupied with the past, or are not open to a future that may dash the status quo against the rocks of the beachhead of the "kin-dom" of God. However, this is the very place that people of faith are being called to during a crisis. How they respond will determine whether their faith will fall by the side or whether it will serve as a new platform which will help them stand on their own two feet supported only by their covenant with God.

And so, as can be surmised from my comments thus far, I believe that prayer, spirituality, and faith can be strong foundations during times of crisis and loss. A living faith can give real life when all possibilities seem dead.

A number of years ago, J.P. Dubois-Dumee reflected on the movement in many people's lives toward a spiritual renewal—in particular a renewal of prayer. He felt that when one looks at the desire to make one's faith come alive through prayer and attention to one's faith, one can detect among other things:

a need for permanence in a civilization of transience;

a need for the Absolute when all else has become relative;

a need for silence in the midst of noise;

a need for gratuitousness in the face of unbelievable greed;

a need for poverty amid the flaunting of wealth;

a need for contemplation in a century of action, for without contemplation, action risks becoming mere agitation;

a need for communication in a universe content with entertainment and sensationalism;

a need for peace amid today's universal outbursts of violence;

a need for quality to counterbalance the increasingly prevalent response to quantity;

a need for humility to counteract the arrogance of power and science;

a need for human warmth when everything is being rationalized or computerized;

a need to belong to a small group rather than to be part of a crowd;

a need for slowness to compensate the present eagerness for speed;

a need for truth when the real meaning of words is distorted in political speeches and sometimes even in religious discourses;

a need for transparency when everything seems opaque. Yes, a need for the interior life.[11]

Albert Schweitzer, a profound activist for good, would have probably agreed with these needs. He saw so much sickness, death, poverty, and tragedy. He did so much to alleviate the pain of others. Yet, he also had a foundation of faith that kept him going. But more than that, he saw the foundation of faith as a way to meet social crises and losses as well. Once he said: "One truth stands firm. All that happens in world history rests on something spiritual. If the spiritual is strong, it creates world history. If it is weak, world history suffers."

A covenant of love with God makes it possible to remember healthy self-love when a crisis would normally lead to a loss of self-confidence. A covenant of love with God also makes it possible during times of tragedy to be able to receive love from others so we can return it at a time when normally it would seem that we should only be self-involved. One need only talk to the medical staff who cared for Vice President Hubert Humphrey during his last days to see a clear example of this; they remember less about his needs as a patient and more about his love now that he is gone—he left a legacy of love for them in the way he met his last days fully and generatively.

Seeking Greater Spiritual Resilience and a Healthier Perspective...
• How willing are you to risk putting everything in God's hands? What do you have to lose?

DAY 11

"Ultimately there is no friend who can fully understand us, who can walk with us all the way. We must go forward and walk on our own in response to who we are and who we are called to be in God."

—THOMAS MERTON

Basil Pennington, in his book of reflections on Thomas Merton, talks about Merton's awareness that in the end, we are alone before God:

In his last talk, the one given at the Pan-Asian Monastic Conference in Bangkok, Merton related a story about Chogyam Trungpa Rinpoche. At the critical moment when Rinpoche had to make his decision about leaving Tibet (after a military/political "crackdown" by the Chinese), he found himself isolated in a mountain hut. He did not know what to do. So he sent to a neighboring abbot friend, saying, "What do we do?"

The answer came back: "From now on, Brother, everybody stands on his own two feet." Tom commented that that was an extremely important statement. We all do need some external supports and structures to grow...yet true freedom demands that we be free even from the communities and the structures that support us. Ultimately there is no friend who can fully understand us, who can walk with us all the way. We must go forward and walk on our own in response to who we are and who we are called to be in God.[12]

Pennington also pointed out:

When [Thomas Merton] was preparing an article on the Georgian letters of Boris Pasternak, he spoke to the community at Gethsemane about them. He pointed out and commented at length on a particular statement in the last of the letters written shortly before Pasternak's death (in which he said): "Everywhere in the world one has to pay for the right to live on one's naked spiritual reserves."[13]

Pennington believes as Merton does that the cost is great to come to this point of complete freedom and that Merton was willing to pay the price. The question is: Are we? I think that people with deep faith are. And during periods of crisis and loss, it is this very deep faith, this covenant with God, which helps them deal with doubt and work through cynicism. In addition, it sets the stage for them to increase self-awareness and self-esteem at the very time when the movement of a crisis is trying to make them crumble.

Seeking Greater Spiritual Resilience and a Healthier Perspective...
- Do you rely on others for spiritual strength to such an extent that you have no reserves of your own? How might you strengthen your own faith?

DAY 12

Depression often occurs when we have forgotten to love the presence of God in all living things—including, maybe *especially*, in ourselves.

A crisis can lead to a point where the usual sources of self-esteem are eroded and one is left naked and vulnerable. When we are in the midst of a crisis, we certainly don't see a clear way out. We feel like the deep-sea diver who had scarcely reached the ocean floor when a message which left him in a dilemma came from the surface. It said: "Come up quickly…the ship is sinking!"

We are all loyal to at least one negative view of ourselves. It is the deep negative belief that cognitive therapists speak about or the driving unconscious force from early in life that the dynamically oriented psychotherapists focus on in their work. Depression often occurs when we have forgotten to love the presence of God in ourselves.

Self-awareness and healthy self-love go hand in hand. If anything, spiritual self-awareness is really a religious way of viewing self-confidence because it is a self-confidence not built on lies we have told ourselves but on an appreciation of the footprints of God in our own personality and an understanding of how we often block those footprints from becoming clear to ourselves and others.

Sartre has been quoted as saying that to live well is difficult and yet possible. For the person of faith this becomes truly possible in a crisis through the reception of God's grace. The fascinating theologian Rudolf Bultmann once noted:

> God's grace is to [a person's] grace in such a thoroughgoing sense that it supports the whole of [a person's] existence, and can only be conceived of as grace by those who surrender their whole existence and let themselves fall into the unfathomable dizzy depths without seeking for something to hold on to.[14]

Several years ago something happened to me that made Bultmann's point painfully clear to me. I was asked to do a series of lectures for a group of people who had very low morale. This request was not surprising in itself because I am often requested to go into difficult situations and to present the truth in a way that new possibilities and hopes can spring from the psychological and spiritual ashes of hurt feelings, discarded religious structures, and the stress which expectations to live one's individual and community life in new ways naturally brings with it.

The surprising thing for me was that nothing seemed to work. Not only did the group seem to hate me before I arrived, but they also appeared to hold onto this feeling during the period that I was working with them. The result was that I began to feel insecure, anxious, somewhat depressed, and angry. And this was reflected in my prayer life as well.

In my time spent alone with God, I asked to be relieved of the situation. (At some level, I think I also wished I could pray an Old Testament prayer: "Smite all of these people, their families, friends, even their children!" However, I knew God would say, "We don't do that anymore, Bob!")

The response that I seemed to receive to my prayers did not really appear to be an answer at the time. The sense I got in prayer was that God was asking me whether I thought I had discerned properly that coming to this situation was in fact God's will and not simply my desire to perform in a spectacular fashion. I responded in prayer affirmatively. Then God seemed to say to me: "Then why are all of these complaints relevant? People did terrible things to me when I obeyed my Father, and many years ago I also told you that on occasion they would do the same, if not worse, to you if you chose to pick up your cross, be obedient, and follow me."

What could I say after sensing this response from God? I realized that I had become so used to people appreciating my ministry of teaching that when the going got rough, as Jesus had warned me might happen long ago, I had a hard time with it. I was more concerned with my image than in simply being faithful to the call to serve and be in solidarity with these troubled and pressured people.

One of the positive outcomes of all of this, however, was that I think I care a little less now about my image and can spend more of my energy seeing whether I am responding to God as I am being called each day or following my anxious ego's continuous demand to inflate or protect itself.

So, in the case of a person of faith, while a crisis may be just as painful, it can, as Rabbi Kushner pointed out in his wonderful book *When Bad Things Happen to Good People*, lead to growth rather than bitterness. The guidance comes from being in touch with God. And the choice is usually up to us whether we will avail ourselves of such help. Maybe that is why small and large difficulties in life are the painful "crossroads" in which our faith can either atrophy or grow dramatically.

Seeking Greater Spiritual Resilience and a Healthier Perspective...

- Reflect on a time when you felt like a failure. Were you relying too much on yourself and too little on God?

DAY 13

"Education is the ability to listen to almost anything without losing your temper or self-confidence."

—ROBERT FROST

A spirituality that recognizes we are always special in the eyes of God and that the so-called "specialness in the eyes of the world" is nonexistent, or at best fleeting, but it helps us to appreciate what a crisis can teach us. As was emphasized above, Robert Frost once made the comment: "Education is the ability to listen to almost anything without losing your temper or your self-confidence."

We are very tied to our image, and often we don't even know it or for that matter appreciate how temporary and illusory trying to hold on to or put faith in our image can be. I remember a small event that happened several years ago which I try to recall anytime I feel myself losing perspective with respect to my own image.

I had been asked by a colleague to give a workshop at a government installation for Veterans' Administration employees. After a longer drive than I had expected, I arrived at the base feeling a bit annoyed. But all of my annoyance lifted and was replaced by pride when I noticed a large marquee by the front gate which bore the following message in three-foot letters: "WELCOME DR. ROBERT WICKS!" I thought to myself: "Oh, how I wish I had a camera so I could take a picture of this for my mother." (Never mind my wife, I regressed all the way back into childhood!) Then I drove over to a large theater which looked as though it could hold thousands. As I got out and walked toward the large hall, I thought to myself: "I did not realize how famous I was; this important address to such a large group could be my finest hour." Then when I got inside, there were only twelve people there waiting for me to speak. I guess God was trying to keep me and my ego in conversation!

Seeking Greater Spiritual Resilience and a Healthier Perspective...

- At the best of times, we have a realistic sense of who we are and what gifts we offer to the world. How do our difficult days and the crises of our lives show us where we have lost our perspective?

DAY 14

"The day will come when, after mastering the ether, the winds, the tides, gravity, we shall master the energies of love for God. And then, for the second time in the history of the world, [people] will have made fire [their] servant."

—Pierre Teilhard de Chardin

Chardin is referring to the "fire" of faith which is the mark of spiritual resilience. This is the fire that can burn no matter what darkness comes. And like the ever-present hot pot of tea the Irish have warming on their stoves to help guard against the chill of a cold, rainy winter afternoon, a strong faith stands by constantly, although quietly at times, waiting to warm us down deep so we can remember.

Remember what? Remember the covenant. Remember grace. And remember that the sun is not gone forever and the clouds are not permanent…only the presence of God is eternal.

Many spiritual leaders have ceased to be surprised by the Bible. The simple reality is that religious people always know how the stories turn out. As a result, the challenge of the Spirit is set aside and the perspective, which might come with an ongoing, actual dialogue with the word, is lost as well.

Many of us, in our effort to become thoroughly familiar on a cognitive level with scripture, have lost Karl Barth's sense that when you are asking the Bible, "What is this book saying?" it should answer: "Who is this that is asking?" Still, when the interplay between personal identity and the living word is missing, this sense of an ongoing formation of biblical identity is lost as well. It is no wonder that a number of years ago William Sloan Coffin, in his usually colorful fashion, said: "The Bible is like a mirror. When an ass peers in, don't expect an apostle to peer out."

What can we do about this? Well, the practical recommendation here is to read sacred scripture each day as usual, but at least part of the time, do it in the spirit of the practice of *lectio divina*. By that I mean we should: (1) select a few minutes each day to read the scriptures prayerfully and with a sense of expectation and surprise. Such an approach breaks down the common modes of imagery and allows us to see more vividly those themes that previously remained in the shadows and were unable to prophetically challenge us. (2) While reading the passages, do a spiritual exegesis; that is, read the words with love and a sense of discovery until something seems to strike home. (3) Simply sit with that passage as one would with a good friend—not thinking, analyzing (or, heaven forbid, creating a lecture or homily out of it!), but instead remaining in a quiet, listening spirit so the word can nurture and challenge you.

Seeking Greater Spiritual Resilience and a Healthier Perspective…

- The busiest people among us can find fifteen or twenty minutes each week for something that is truly important. If you aren't already doing so, set aside time during your day to read and reflect on the Word of God.

PART TWO

Uncovering and Addressing the Enemies
of a Healthy Spiritual and Psychological Perspective

The call to seek and maintain a healthier perspective in life, which represents the core of spiritual resilience, is a call to both be mature personally and in community. It is a call to forsake both passivity and willfulness in our movement toward personal and communal development. And to respond to this simple but difficult call, we must do all in our power to flow with the grace of God by uncovering and dealing with the enemies of perspective that assail us at every turn. Three of the major ones I would like to present here are:

- self-esteem problems
- anxieties due to an inordinate fear of failure, doubt, and change
- a pollution of our spirit due to negativity

DAY 15

"Remember that you must build your life as if it were a work of art."

—ABRAHAM HESCHEL

In 1972, a little over a week before the great Rabbi Abraham Heschel died, he was asked by an interviewer for NBC-TV if he had a message for today's youth. Rather than being put off by such a broad and challenging question, he nodded affirmatively and said: "Remember, that there is meaning beyond absurdity. Know that every deed counts, that every word is power...above all, remember that you must build your life as if it were a work of art."[15]

His words to the young then should still be a calling cry not only to the young but to all of us no matter our age. However, knowing a worthy goal such as this, and being able to fulfill it on a daily basis, are two radically different things. There are many blocks to spiritual and psychological perspective that must be unmasked and dealt with every day. Otherwise, the gift of perspective God offers anew each day so we can remain spiritually resilient will remain unwrapped and unused, and we will be beleaguered by unnecessary worries, doubts, and anxieties. The result: confusion instead of clarity, passivity in lieu of passion, and withdrawal in place of solidarity with others. In such instances, rather than building our life as if it were a work of art, we will feel wrecked in emotions that will tell us we are lost, overwhelmed, and unsettled.

For all of us, the call to spiritual and psychological perspective is both a feminine and masculine one. From a "masculine orientation" we have traditionally been called psychologically to separate, individuate, and be mature adults according to the theme of 1 Corinthians 12, which calls us to discover and prize the uniqueness we have to contribute to the world. The spiritual goal, from such a vantage point then, is obedience to God's call to be all that we can be as persons made in the image and likeness of God; at its core it is a cognitive call to try to think, perceive, and understand who God wants us to be and what the Lord wants us to do in life.

However, this is not possible unless we also heed the feminine call to psychological affiliation and spiritual solidarity. We can't go to God alone; if and when we try, the dangers are great. Withdrawal and isolation can easily masquerade as solidarity with God; religious elitism can often be touted and supported as if it were real piety; and an absence of affect, which can leave us feeling emotionally sterile, may be inappropriately seen positively as true "detachment" or "ascesis," which it never is.

Seeking Greater Spiritual Resilience and a Healthier Perspective...
- Artists often take a step back from their work to see it from a new perspective. Look at your life from the perspective of some of the people with whom you interact each day. How might they see you? How is that different from the way you see yourself? How might that add to your own spiritual resilience in ways that allow you to reach out to others in a stronger, more helpful way?

DAY 16

One of the greatest things we can do for others is to learn to like ourselves. People with solid self-esteem are less defensive, are better able to deal with the negativity and pain of others, and are in a good position to inspire true hope in others.

Some people are fully human—so much so that when we are with them we feel very peaceful, accepted...it is all right for us to be ourselves. In their presence we seem to breathe more easily, speak more freely, and smile more naturally. It is as if we didn't age during the time we were with them because we felt too relaxed to wear out—even a little.

Then after leaving them we feel some regret. To be with them again would be great. Even better! To be more like them ourselves, to be real, to be open, to be free to be ourselves in all types of situations with all kinds of people, wouldn't that be just wonderful! Not only would this be a personally peaceful way of life, it would be pure gift for others because one of the greatest things we can do for others is to learn to like ourselves. I don't mean love ourselves—that's too philosophical. I mean like ourselves—get a kick out of ourselves!

Here's an example. I remember being "in love" in junior high school. Her name was Pam. She was marvelous. There was only one problem:

I couldn't tell anyone because she wasn't the type one was allowed to fall head over heels in love with. In adolescence, one's "loves" are like mirrors. They have to look a certain way because the important thing is how you look standing next to them. Now Pam was attractive to me but she didn't look the part as dictated by the norm informally set out by my friends (not tall enough or the right color hair), so I tried to hide my feelings for fear of being ostracized—a terrible thing for me at fifteen!

Yet, in my heart I liked her in spite of it all and occasionally it showed. This resulted in a few close calls with respect to my friends. However, it wasn't until just a few years ago when I was reminiscing about school that I remembered this part of my life and finally realized why I liked Pam so much. It was because she liked—really liked herself. Not in a narcissistic way, but almost in a fun way. She got a kick out of Pam. She enjoyed being herself and being spontaneous with others. She seemed to like who she was and who she was becoming. This provided a lift for me and I'm sure for others who knew her then and probably now as well.

The reason why this type of attitude would be helpful to others rather than being merely narcissistic is clear. People with solid self-esteem are less defensive. Because they do not accept all criticism as fact, they are better able to deal with the pain and negativity of others. Their attitude also places them in a good position to inspire true hope in others.

Seeking Greater Spiritual Resilience and a Healthier Perspective…
- When we're going through tough times, we begin to feel as though everyone is against us. Think about a time when you may have done this. Is it really you disliking yourself that's at work here? How can that awareness help you change your approach?

DAY 17

> People who know and are at peace with themselves always have something to share no matter how difficult the situation turns out to be.

People who know themselves, are spiritually resilient, and are at peace with themselves always have something to share, no matter how difficult the situation turns out to be. They are alive, and those who encounter them enjoy the possibility of living clearer, more meaningful lives because of the gentle open space they offer. (This is the general principle behind such processes as psychotherapy and spiritual direction and guidance.)

People who are in touch with their own gifts, are grateful to God for them (this is an especially important aspect), and seek to nurture them are like oases for the worried, anxious, poor, depressed, and oppressed of the world. They are a place of refuge. In some cases, for some reason, persons like this seem to do it naturally. And so, they may not be conscious of being this way themselves or be very noticeable to others. In addition, age is not a factor; people like this thrive and encourage others at each level of human development.

This lesson was brought closer to home several years ago when I was teaching at a local Franciscan college. Its president—who was also a psychologist—was resigning. We were sitting in her office and saying our good-byes. I told her that her greatest gift to me was her ability to forgive. Since sometimes I was impetuous, in my intensity and involvement I had occasionally said and done things that were somewhat painful for her. Yet, although we had had our differences, she had repeatedly wiped the slate clean, and for this I told her I was very grateful.

In response, she said that she wanted to share with me what she felt was one of my greatest gifts. She said, "No matter how many things you have written, no matter how much you have accomplished or become well known in certain circles, you have never lost your childlike nature with respect to yourself. You seem always to be surprised and to enjoy the new things you find out about yourself." And what she said stuck with me because, although it may not sound like much, it was one of the most important compliments I had ever received.

This comment is a benchmark statement for me with respect to mental health and spiritual wisdom. To be unrelentingly open with respect to oneself is the lifelong goal of self-knowledge and self-esteem. I believe that from a psychological perspective one of the most serious sins is to ignore, deny, or worship our own personalities rather than to prize them, find out all about them, and seek to express them naturally and freely with a sense of *mitzvah* (giving and expecting nothing in return). To have a sense of awe about the presence of God everywhere, including (maybe especially) oneself, changes the way one leads one's life.

Seeking Greater Spiritual Resilience and a Healthier Perspective…
- Reflect on your gifts, those things that you can offer to others and to the world. What one thing can you do today to develop those gifts and be more certain of their true value?

DAY 18

Failure can awaken us to life in a much more dramatic way than success ever could.

Possessing a healthy perspective is an essential key to psychological and spiritual resilience and wholeness. If our attitude is healthy and our spirit sound, then whom shall we fear? In common parlance, how long must we worry unnecessarily? Why should we be upset for longer than is normal when we face the difficulties of daily life?

One theologian once suggested that we replace the word *faith* in the scriptures with the word *trust*. In such a scenario, failure, doubt, and change will lead us to a greater rather than lesser faith. An attitude built on trust (in other words, an attitude of hope built on a living faith) can change how we see and experience everything—including even normally defeating events. In Christ's words: "If your eye is sound, your whole body will be full of light" (Matthew 6:22).

Embarrassment and awkwardness are the handles that God's redemptive grace holds onto. When failure shakes us, it is really shaking our false images, not our true selves. God doesn't call us to be successful (that's a secular command). God simply calls us to respond. Knowing this lesson of grace and God's gratuitousness is essential if we wish to be caring Christians. The more we are involved in God's work, and the bigger our world of interactions becomes, the more we are apt to make mistakes and have the natural inclination to pull back.

And yet, even if we succumb to our anxieties and try to withdraw, we won't feel peace; withdrawal offers no guarantee of security. As the humorist Robert Benchley wryly noted: "My only solution for the problem of habitual accidents…is for everybody to stay in bed all day. Even then, there is always the chance that you will fall out."

Fear of doubt is another enemy of spiritual and psychological perspective. Former Secretary of State John Foster Dulles once said: "If you are scared to go to the brink, you are lost." The same can be said of faith. Faith that does not include risk is often a sham.

Seeking Greater Spiritual Resilience and a Healthier Perspective…
- What situations do you avoid because they seem too risky? Select one that you suspect could lead to spiritual growth and find a way to make it part of your life.

DAY 19

> Although we can encounter God everywhere, one of the best
> places to meet the Lord is contemplatively in the void.

In stillness, in silence, in solitude, we become frightened. We look either for something to hold onto or for something to fill us. We may turn to prayer, seeking structure, results, or a proven way. But such prayer is actually a flight from the void rather than a contemplative acceptance of it. This goes counter to the call to let go, "simply" be ourselves, and meet God in a real, unique relationship.

In reflecting on the spirituality of Thomas Merton, James Finley writes: "Looking for God is like seeking a path in a field of snow; if there is no path and you are looking for one, walk across it and there is your path."[16]

The void challenges us, despite our distractions, to see things and God as they are.

A tendency toward spiritual romanticism is something we would rather forget. Let me change that: It is something I frequently would like to forget. It is not surprising then that James Finley once again says the following about Thomas Merton to serve as a reminder to us about this danger:

Merton's life was not a romantic adventure…. He woke before dawn with a mind "not totally reconciled to being out of bed." He ate, worked, walked in the woods and prayed. In the winter he was cold and in the summer he was hot. And that is the true self. It is the self that is nobody, that is ordinary and poor. It is this ordinary self that is extraordinary for it is this ordinary self [that is] one with the moment, one with the concrete reality of everyday life, that is the self God creates, the poor self made rich in the poverty of the cross.[17]

Seeking Greater Spiritual Resilience and a Healthier Perspective…

• When are you tempted to turn your faith into a kind of spiritual romanticism? How might you keep it rooted in reality instead?

DAY 20

Our depressive, anxious, stressful feelings are sometimes the result of our putting our psychological and spiritual "hands" around something less than God.

Instead of just sitting in silence and solitude with God, facing our boredom, lack of control, loneliness, and inner fragmentation, our prayer tends to become mechanical. In our lives too, we try to fill the void with addictions: to work, food, drugs, alcohol, worry, money, power, order, the church…yes, even prayer.

In one of my trips outside of the United States I came face to face with this issue. Having flown for hours, I was picked up at the airport and deposited at a hotel. After unpacking, I sat on the edge of the bed and looked around the room. It was clean and sparse. After a few minutes I began to feel lonely and empty. I even thought: "What if I died here; no one would really know me or feel awful about it." When I experienced this depressive thinking, my first inclination as a good psychologist was to simply tell myself that this was depressive thinking and to distract myself by calling or writing someone, or by reading one of the books I had brought with me.

But then I realized that although this would temporarily lift the depression I was experiencing, it would do little for me in the long run.

I would not be dealing with the underlying cause for my loneliness and dark thoughts. When I would be in a situation like this again, I would be lonely again. Nothing would have changed. So, instead I sat with, and in, the void. But this time I was alone with my thoughts and with God.

At first my situation seemed to get worse. I began to see my own finitude, to appreciate the ugly truths about myself, and to feel helpless that I had no real answers to the big questions in the world. I began to get in touch with my feelings of alienation and anxiety about being a stranger, among people whom I did not know and who did not know me. Finally, after a while, I had the strange feeling that it would be all right. By facing my own lies about myself, my inability to control things, my sense of being a charlatan before a loving God, I could begin to be free. I could be free to accept God's love and to embrace this painful but liberating truth: in the eyes of the world I shall never be seen as special for any length of time, yet in the eyes of the Lord I am always special.

This lesson of grace helped me to be more open to myself and the new people I met on this trip. I greeted them as unknown friends instead of frightening strangers. I also began to see the danger of the "spiritual romanticism" that remains present even at times when I profess to be interested in being in real relationship with God.

Seeking Greater Spiritual Resilience and a Healthier Perspective…
- Prayer and pious devotions can sometimes be as much a way of avoiding a relationship with God as seeking that relationship. What are some ways you hide from God?

DAY 21

"I pray to God to free me of God for God's sake."
—Meister Eckhart

An inordinate fear of change is another block to spiritual resilience that is marked by having a healthy perspective in life. Change can break through comfortable familiarity and uncover prejudice. Jesus called for a new loyalty that would put God above others, no matter who they are in our lives (Mt 11:37). Too often we form God in our own image rather than being open to a growing presence of God in us and the world at large. It's no wonder then that in the early fourteenth century, Meister Eckhart noted, "I pray to God to free me of God, for God's sake."

Celie, the central character in the novel *The Color Purple*, is told "You can't see anything at all until you get man off your eyeball."[18] It is at this point in the story that Celie is handcuffed by her image of God as an old, uncaring, white male with whom she can't relate, rather than seeing God as the living God who calls her to be in relationship. This is what we call "spirituality."

Change often unmasks our delusions, the scenarios we set up in which God protects us in our comfortability. In the events that occur on the road to Emmaus (Luke 24), it is this theme which comes through.

We begin to recognize that the spiritual journey, if we may call it that, is a journey of *unlearning*. In the spirit of John of the Cross in his Ascent of Mount Carmel, we recognize the value of change in our journey to God: "The more darkness it causes, the greater light it gives." From this vantage point, confusion is not bad if it brings with it greater concern and increases our willingness to learn what God may be teaching us, what space for the Divine God is making within us, and where God may be leading us next.

I think that no matter how we take care of ourselves, such instances will overtake us. Paradoxically, they can be graced moments. If we let them, they can bring us back to the recognition that we are called neither to win nor to abandon the fight to rid the world of darkness. We are not the ones called to affect a cure. We are only called to be present and to do what we can. At times like these, we must try to deal with our own "negative grandiosity." We must seek to deflate our "savior complex," our desire to be spectacular, to have an impact. We must recognize our temptation to "go it alone," and our own negative thinking when we fail. We must also be aware of what good things are taking place in the world, our world, and to sit with our negativity and desires to control things. In a gentle way we must begin to see what can be learned from the kind of thinking which has produced such distressful feelings.

Often we try either to run away from our own feelings of despair or to conquer them. We need to stay with them—in Jungian terms, to make friends with what is just beyond our awareness in our "shadow"— to see what can come out of the darkness for us. At the very least, we will begin to see how we have relied too much on ourselves and that, in focusing on the problems of the world, we have forgotten to see what is right in it. A short story by a Vietnamese Zen Roshi points this out. He said: "During the [Vietnam] war, we were so busy helping the wounded that we sometimes forgot to smell the flowers. Night has a very pleasant smell [in Vietnam], especially in the country. But we would forget to pay attention to the smell of mint, coriander, thyme, and sage."[19]

Seeking Greater Spiritual Resilience and a Healthier Perspective...
- What is your instinctive reaction to confusion, doubt, and change? How might you become more aware of God in the changes inevitable in any life?

DAY 22

Sometimes we allow the negativity that surrounds us to become part of our own outlook to an unhealthy degree.

Another enemy of a healthier psychological and spiritual perspective that forms the core of a strong spiritual resilience is the negativity that infects us due to the great frustration and sadness we encounter in the world. In being a caring parent, family member, friend, coworker, or minister, it is impossible for us not to be affected by the pain and helplessness of others.

Several years ago I remember returning home after a day of seeing patients in my private practice. When I came in, my wife, Michaele, asked me how my day was. In response I was ready to say, "Fine" (which is what most of us say almost automatically no matter how things really are). But I was overcome with such a deep sense of sadness that I said, "Terrible." She replied by asking: "Why, what happened?" Looking at her, I sat down on the kitchen chair without taking off my raincoat. Then as I have taught others, I reviewed the day to see what had happened, what I had blown out of proportion, what negative belief I was allowing to get hold of me.

And then I recognized what it was. It was not one specific event, it was a series of almost unrecognized ones. It was not some great problem

I had to deal with that day. Instead, as I sat there reflecting, I began to see that over the past weeks, without realizing it, I had begun to absorb people's anxieties, sadness, helplessness, and hopelessness until I could no longer continue to help them. The abuse, loneliness, financial and marital difficulties, sexual addictions, interpersonal rebuffs, angers, and hardships had all been absorbed by me over time. I felt slowly defeated by them and, to be honest, just felt like crying. I could now fully appreciate what a woman once shared with me in a reflection paper: "I am amazed that so much sadness could fit into my body."

One of the surest ways to let negativity get hold of us is not to take care of ourselves. I try to make sure I get enough rest, food, and exercise and have enough supportive people in my life. Then when people come to me to hear a presentation or ask for some advice, I am healthy enough to be really available to them. I want them to feel that they can drop anything on me without having to worry about me, that they can even be angry, contentious, or in a panic, and I will be free enough to help. Still, this attitude is not really a popular one, especially in Christian circles. There is a great call for people who are involved to look overworked and be overburdened. When you don't fit into this category, people are thrown off by it.

Once I was on a trip out of the United States to teach for a week. Afterward I planned to teach in Vermont for several weeks. Knowing this, one person said to me: "You poor thing, you really are overworked." Puzzled, I responded, "I'm not sure what you mean." She went on to explain that she thought I must be exhausted from teaching every day for a week in her country. To this I responded that I was really enjoying myself; the challenge was a good one. Not to be undone by this, she said "But you will be going back to teach after this, won't you?" I answered:

"Yes, but I will have a week off between here and my teaching in Vermont." Still, she pressed on with her point: "But after teaching there for three weeks, you will certainly be exhausted." I responded to this as well by pointing out that I would have weekends off in Vermont and was taking a week at Martha's Vineyard after that as my official vacation. This seemed to stop her, but after a short pause her attitude seemed to completely shift in the other direction, and her eyes seemed to now say: "My heavens, but you certainly take a lot of time off!" I guess there's not much room in church circles for people who shun Christian masochism.

Another aspect of taking care of ourselves is to have supportive people in our lives. A number of these have to take empathic, teaching roles, but certainly among them are those loyal people who will let us know in no uncertain terms that they are behind us.

In being committed Christians we will always have the *prophets* in our lives who will keep us on the track. Not to have such people to call us to be all that we can be and to challenge us when we stray from the path is very dangerous. But I think it is almost equally dangerous not to have very *sympathetic people*—real cheerleaders—in our lives who encourage us fully at every turn. I always tease people, particularly those in ministry, that they need the kind of individuals who, in response to our complaints about others, give us so much support that we almost feel guilty. And when we express some annoyance at a person or persons, they say something like: "You are totally right, and they are totally wrong. As a matter of fact, I am getting on my knees this very moment to pray for their early happy death!"

Behind my silly musings there is a serious point: we can't go it alone. We need a balance of support. We need criticism and feedback as much as we need encouragement and acceptance. Without such a balance, we face the twin challenges of either going on our own "Christian safari," thinking we are doing God's will, of being crushed under the crosses of commitment that can only be held up when we are part of a supportive community of believers. As Henri Nouwen recognizes: "We can take a lot of physical and even mental pain when we know that it truly makes us a part of the life we live together in the world. But when we feel cut off from the human family, we quickly lose heart."[20]

Seeking Greater Spiritual Resilience and a Healthier Perspective...

• Where do you find support during difficult times? Who nourishes your spirit?

DAY 23

One way to look at a spiritually resilient life marked by a healthy perspective is to see it as a simple life of possibilities.

Maxim Gorky, in his autobiography, quoted his grandfather: "'In my days dresses were far richer and finer than they are today,' he would say. 'They spent more on dresses then, but lived more simply, peacefully.'"[21] I feel this quote is reflective of what the spiritual life is all about. The spiritual life is not so much about filling oneself with love or special reinforcing positive experiences but instead allowing the love we already have to blossom. With such an attitude, inconsequential concerns lose their power so the possibilities of God can surface. The simple and peaceful life can offer rich encounters with the ultimate if we don't prejudge how God will be made manifest to us. Not knowing how God will appear in us and before us we must move ahead with what seems good and look everywhere to see what good may be happening right in front of us almost without our noticing it. Let me offer a couple of examples.

Several years ago on television in Ireland there was a show that was called *The Gay Byrne Hour*. Some loved it, some hated it but almost everyone watched it. One of the special features of the show around Christmas time was the live Christmas Eve broadcast held outside on Grafton Street (the main road running through Dublin). During this particular show the host would invite people to sing, tell stories, and interact with him. One Christmas, knowing this was to happen, a young woman convinced her friend to go with her to Grafton Street and try to get on the show. She had a good voice and thought it would be fun to test her talent in a live broadcast, never expecting the chance would present itself.

So she and her friend went. Then, much to her surprise and delight, she was chosen out of the crowd and asked if she would be interested in telling a story or singing something. She said she would and she started singing "O Holy Night." People who were present said that as she began to sing, all of Grafton Street went silent. One person living in Ireland at the time claimed to me that he felt almost all of Ireland went silent. One voice. No expectations. A profound impact. The unexpected hand of God in the ordinary. Never could this woman have expected the impact she would have. We can't predict the hour we will be called or how God will call us to be a light for others.[22]

The same can be said of the possibilities in the world for us to experience God in others. This was particularly brought across to me at the conclusion of the liturgy celebrated to mark the bicentennial of the Baltimore Carmel—the oldest Carmel in the United States. As the liturgy was drawing to a close, the choir began to sing the Hallelujah Chorus of Handel's *Messiah*. As I listened to them, I was distracted by some peripheral motion. When I looked over to the side I could see that there was a group of hearing-impaired persons who had come to the celebration. And much to my surprise, their leader knew the words to the chorus and was singing it for those in front of him. Then, of even greater surprise to me, the hearing impaired section of the congregation began to sign it with him. (They knew it too!) As I watched them and heard the choir in the background, I was overwhelmed. After it was over I knew that I had never heard nor been as moved by Handel's work as I was at this moment. The hand of God had moved me to hear the Spirit in a new way.

Too often we say God is missing—both in ourselves and in the world. Too frequently we lose both our spiritual and our psychological perspective and wish that something dramatic would return it to us. Yet, more often than not, our epiphanies rely on the ordinary. It is in being awake to the presence of God both in our movements toward maturity and affiliation, and toward obedience and solidarity, that the possibilities which are now hidden from us can be revealed. Knowing this is the gift of understanding; practicing it every day is openness to the gift of insight. There is a world of difference between these two gifts, and how we experience life will surely prove this to us.

Seeking Greater Resilience and a Healthier Perspective...
• Be alert for epiphanies in the most ordinary events of your day. Sometimes awareness is all that's missing.

PART THREE

Reaching Out…
Without Being Pulled Down

"But those who identify the kingdom of God with heaven are mistaken; the kingdom means rather the spiritual life, which begins in this life by faith, and in which we grow deeply as we progress in constant faith."[23]

—JOHN CALVIN ON JOHN 3:3

Most committed Christians would not quibble with the claim that a life of service to others in the light of the gospel can be quite dangerous to one's emotional and spiritual health. The question for many of us remains: "While we are extending our warmth to others, how do we prevent our own emotional flame from burning out in the process?"

Possibly one of the reasons this question is still a pressing one is that while a knowledge of the psychology of stress is important, at a deeper level, a more significant way of balancing and strengthening one's efforts to care for others in need is by taking the necessary steps to try to center those efforts spiritually. One's efforts and actions on behalf of others must be based not on one's own abilities or knowledge, but instead on a *covenantal* spirituality. This is a radical openness to a prayerful relationship with the presence of God in oneself, in others, and in those quiet honest encounters with the Lord in silence and solitude.

When people approach us for help, no matter what they are seeking, they are also really—to some degree—saying: "[Please,] we would like to see Jesus" (John 12:21). And, as in the time of the original apostles, when we recognize this significant element in the questions people are asking, we naturally feel overwhelmed and turn to Jesus as they did. And, as in the case of the historical Jesus, the Lord today returns the burden to us, giving us the command: "You give them something to eat" (Mark 6:37).

And so, an essential question for us to ask of ourselves at this point is: What in fact do *I* have to give those who come to us for spiritual food? Our reply to this question may well determine whether our response will be truly authentic, and whether, in the long run, we will be able to sustain "the good fight" or burn out before the job is done.

DAY 24

Our faith and our spirituality must always be more than mere knowledge; it needs to be an active covenant (deep relationship) with God.

In all that we do in service to the Gospel, we must share a sense of the passion and perspective of Christ with others. And this is primarily centered in only one place: in a covenantal spirituality based on a deep living faith received from God. Anything less than this, as John Wesley notes in the following statement, falls short of the mark:

> I had a sort of faith during my early life. But devils also have a sort of faith. Still, neither they nor I received the faith of the covenant of promise. Even the apostles had a sort of faith when they were first with Jesus in Cana. Then and there, they "believed in him" in a way. But they did not yet have the faith which overcomes the world.[24]

Consequently, we must take the necessary steps to continually develop our spiritual openness so that our prayer life does not remain narrow and our daily prayerful interactions with others don't become distorted. We need to nurture a radical relationship with the living God and to show gratitude to the Lord for the gift of grace (so that we don't unconsciously make Christian action into just another performance-oriented activity). The next several days' reflections will help us avoid modeling our own lives in accord with a world that glorifies success. Instead, we will strive to recall our covenant with God and respond to life in obedience to God and solidarity with others.

A sound covenantal spirituality is based in part on self-knowledge. There must be a willingness to face the natural resistances we have to uncovering unpleasant truths about ourselves and to deal with the more subtle "sins of adaptation" that occur when we unconsciously seek to make the Christian message comfortable.

As we can see in the following comment, John Calvin strongly believed in self-knowledge:

> With good reason the ancient proverb [Know thyself] strongly recommended knowledge of self. For if it is considered disgraceful for us not to know all that pertains to the business of human life, even more detestable is our ignorance of ourselves, by which, when making decisions in necessary matters, we miserably deceive and even blind ourselves.[25]

In addition, Calvin recognized that true self-knowledge was not self-worship, as some of the current narcissistic self-help literature would have us believe. Instead, it is the font of true humility. In his commentary on Isaiah 6:5, he noted: "Until God reveals himself to us, we do not think we are [persons]… we think we are gods; but when we have seen God, then we begin to feel and know what we are. Hence springs true humility, which consists in this, that a [person] make no claim for himself [herself], and depend wholly on God."[26]

And so, in the spirit of 1 Corinthians 12, self-awareness is important for us not only to begin to appreciate the gifts we are given, but also to recognize the source of those gifts and how we are blocking them from reaching full development, because "from a psychological perspective, sin is primarily the result of denying, ignoring, or worshiping our personality instead of nurturing it in light of the gospel call to respond in faith, hope, and love."[27]

Seeking Greater Spiritual Resilience and a Healthier Perspective...
- Take time today to reflect honestly about your tendency to hide from yourself and from God.

DAY 25

We are seduced by the expectations of others and our own unreasonable expectations rather than the expectations of God.

Most involved Christians happily hold fast to the belief that "Faith without works is dead" (James 2:26). Rarely have I been consulted by a denomination or parish because their pastoral staff or lay leaders were not working hard enough. However, even though this is the case, true acts of love are still hard to find. Acts of compulsion, on the other hand, abound and bind. Most people, especially those in ministry, are unfortunately guilty of that terrible Christian "disease"—chronic niceness. They don't give with a sense of *mitzvah* (giving without expecting anything in return). They give hoping to please and appease.

Giving with a true sense of detachment is a lost art. More often than not, ministry is mainly done with an over-concern about whether people will perceive one's efforts as successful or charitable, and this attitude is a sure road to personal or ministerial "burnout."

Urban Holmes especially appreciated this theme in his book *Spirituality for Ministry* where he noted: "The opposite of detachment is not compassion, it is seduction."[28] We are seduced by the expectations of others and our own unreasonable expectations rather than the expectations of God. Too often we give without discerning whether or not God is calling us to carry certain crosses. When this occurs, such undisciplined activism may lead to an unnecessary depletion of our resources and a cessation of vital involvement in ministry. Christian masochism is still masochism.

The reasons for such self-destructive actions are myriad, but certainly they must include concern about what people will think, concern about one's image as an involved Christian. Yet this worrisome attitude about how one looks, and whether one is pleasing others, goes completely counter to Christ's example in his ministry. For nowhere in the New Testament is there evidence of Jesus comparing himself to others or clinging to his divinity. Instead, he was only interested in obeying the Father and being in solidarity with others.

Jesus knew he was loved; in common parlance, he did not have a self-esteem problem. He did not give to others in order to be loved. Rather, he gave because *he was in love*. Therefore, one of the most dramatic steps you can take in becoming a person who is more generous with others is to learn to like yourself and to appreciate that you are a special creation of God entirely independent of the world's view.

Seeking Greater Spiritual Resilience and a Healthier Perspective...

• How does a deep belief that God loves you affect your relationship with others?

DAY 26

"Most of the trouble in the world is caused by people wanting to be important."

—T.S. Eliot

If Eliot is right about this, then the reality we should model is: Because of Christ's love, we are already important. In reaching out to others, this need to be important is sometimes disguised; it can be seen under the garb of being liked or being effective or being relevant. Yet, trading passion for popularity results in only short-term rewards. Comfortability and success are never a good substitute for peace. Such peace comes from praying honestly and openly, discerning what God is calling us to do, doing it as best we can, and then not worrying about the results or what people think. To repeat James Fenhagen's important message once again here: "People live cautiously because they pray cautiously."[29]

Ironically, it is the desire to be both cautious and involved that encourages burnout, not the very act of involvement in itself. The simple biblical principle here is that one simply can't serve two masters. Jesus did not say: "It would be nice if you did not serve two masters." He did not say: "You should work against the tendency to serve two masters." He was direct; his command was simple: "You cannot serve two masters" (Matthew 6:24). So, when we try to, we pay the price both psychologically and spiritually.

Having said this, the recommendations I offer for consideration in this area of loving, rather than compulsive, service are:

Continually review your motives for reaching out to others. The Ibo of Nigeria have a saying: "It is the heart that gives; the fingers just let go."[30]

Seek to respond to the Spirit by lighting the one candle God is asking of you at this moment. Appreciate God's sovereignty rather than trying to change the world alone.

Recognize that when your service is leading to depression, despair or anxiety, these "bad fruits" often mean that you have put your hand around something less than God's will (for example, your desire to look good, be spectacular, be loved by others).

Reflect on whether or not you are unconsciously seeking "the crosses" you would prefer over the ones you fear God might be giving you if your life were less hectic and your giving less compulsive.

Seeking Greater Spiritual Resilience and a Healthier Perspective…
- How often do you seek praise rather than doing good for its own sake? How might changing your expectations change the results?

DAY 27

> One of the greatest challenges of the spiritual life is not to give
> love but to receive it.

To grow spiritually and in self-awareness and avoid unnecessarily being
pulled down, feedback from others is also essential. Still, even though
this is the case, we often back away from this process because we are
frightened of what we might hear. This anxiety is an indication once
again that we have centered ourselves on something or someone less
than God. In addition, it is a sign that we have set ourselves up to filter
out the positive and emphasize the negative, to hear praise as a whisper
and negative comments as thunder.

As strange as it sounds, one of the greatest challenges of the spiritual
life is not to give love but to receive it. When we are open to receiving
the love that is all around us, we can freely share it with others and hear
negative criticism without losing perspective or the ability to give. As
John XXIII has been quoted saying, whoever has a heart full of love
always has something to share. Or, as Fr. Michael Scanlan once aptly
observed: "Our communities desperately need justice, non-violence
and self-giving love, but they can only be led to it by those who have it
in themselves."[31]

Feedback should be sought from colleagues who are "soul friends," those spiritually and psychologically mature persons who are not keyed into success and performance, but are willing to expend the energy necessary to listen to us and learn enough about us to be helpful. When we ask others (as the former mayor of New York, Edward Koch, used to), "How am I doing?" we should look to them for concrete helpful comments that will lead us closer to God.

Too often after we finish school, with the absence of a ready community of friends and colleagues (as is especially the case for ordained ministers who were together in the seminary), we try to go it alone. This is a mistake. A community of friends and colleagues and a chance for faith sharing as well as an exchange of views and feelings provide a life in the Spirit necessary for a continued commitment to our work with others in need.

In some cases this need not involve a major time commitment. Good can result in an exchange that takes only minutes. For example, I have felt inspired, challenged, and loved even after a brief encounter with other faculty members and students over lunch.

Informal and formal teaching and preaching also offer good opportunities for information and important feedback for those of us who have the opportunity to be involved in such activities. As Fred Craddock notes: "Preaching is a vital part of pastoral work in that it permits both the preacher and parishioners to weigh, submit to theological examination, integrate, bring to clarity, and express issues that are scattered through the many pastoral contacts and activities."[32]

Discussions after the class or service give an opportunity not just to hear a simple phrase of delight or dissent by others, but a chance to move more deeply into the word.

With the above points in mind, some practical recommendations in the area of feedback I offer for consideration are to

see God's love and hand in the reactions of others;

accept the love that is already around you so you can be nourished to feel strong enough to bear the brunt of necessary criticism;

see the corrections of others as possible doors to a more spiritually vital life and recognize that it is natural to resist change, even good change.

We are all apt to be like Peter and wish to set up tents around beliefs and themes which bring us comfortability and respect—but possibly not God.

Seeking Greater Spiritual Resilience and a Healthier Perspective...

- Do compliments make you more uncomfortable than criticism? How might you develop a healthier approach to *both*?

DAY 28

> "Solitude is not a private therapeutic place. Rather it is a place of conversion, the place where the old self dies, the place where the new self is born, the place where the emergence of the new man and new woman occurs."
>
> —HENRI NOUWEN

We ponder the nuances of Jesus's parables so often that sometimes we forget that he was also frequently very direct in his instruction. When this directness occurs, it is both a duty to obey and an opportunity to try to fathom the deep treasure within the simplicity of the message. One such occasion was the command he gave to his disciples to follow his example: "Come away by yourself to a lonely place, and rest a while" (Mark 6:31).

Since the time of the Lord, this call to "rest in the Lord" (*quies* or *hesychia*) has been emulated by many Christians and most religious leaders. Luther, for example, obeyed this call. We remember him for saying that when he knew he was going to have a very busy day, he would get up even earlier so he could pray longer. He recognized and lived out the desert wisdom maxim: "Prayer quickly straightens out your thoughts."[33] He knew that he needed time to go into his room, shut his door, and pray to the Lord in secret as a way to keep his perspective spiritually centered (Matthew 6:6).

This wisdom is as important today as it was in the time of Christ and in the religiously intense reformation time of Luther. The question then is: Why do we resist giving this time supremacy in our own lives? The answer I offer is that as much as we say we'd like to be filled with the Spirit, we are also frightened of taking on Christ's yoke of peace and perspective because we are unconsciously willful in our desire to control our own destiny (Mt 11:29–30). We want to resist the conversion and the prophetic call that may be heard when we are alone without our badge of works and schedule full of distractions.

As Henri Nouwen points out, solitude is a place of conversion. While I agree with Nouwen's point of view, when I think of the frightening opportunity that silence and solitude bring to listen and to be with the Lord, I am even more drawn to the reflection recently offered by Thomas Long of Princeton Theological Seminary on Paul's Damascus experience:

> When [Paul] describes the Damascus road experience in Galatians, he does so not so much in the language of conversion, but in the classical language of a prophetic call. In other words, the focus is not primarily on something that bubbled up within him, but rather on a claim that came from outside him. He talks less about his becoming alive to Christ than he does about Christ becoming alive to him. To be sure, Paul was transformed by the experience, but before he was transformed, he was transfixed by the presence of the risen Christ. Even in the account of Acts we do not find Paul gliding away from the Damascus road singing the convert's song of a new orientation, "Amazing grace, how sweet the sound.... Once I was blind, but now I see." To the contrary, his song could only have

been, "Amazing grace, how disturbing the presence...once I saw, but now I am blind."[34]

The point is: Paul did not have God...God had Paul! Saul was busy doing "God's work" as best he knew it when the Lord made a claim on him and called him to an opposite mission and an identity he could never have come to by himself.

Maybe that is what we are trying to run from when we make a case for not following Christ's simple call to close the door to be in the room alone with God. Maybe we can appreciate to some degree what Metropolitan Anthony of Sourozh means when he says: "To meet God means to enter into the 'cave of the tiger'—it is not a pussy cat you meet—it's a tiger. The realm of God is dangerous."[35] To say with Samuel, "Speak, Lord. Your servant is listening" (1 Samuel 3:9), is obviously not easy; it's humbling. As Calvin clearly appreciated: "When we have seen God, then we begin to feel and know what we are. Hence springs true humility, which consists in this, that a [person] make no claim for himself [or herself], and depend wholly on God."[36]

Whatever the cost, then, there is no choice if we are to follow Christ's example. Silence and solitude are necessary if we are to hear God's voice. Just as necessary is our willingness to be faithful by giving the Lord the time necessary for quiet prayer each day. How we pray is of course up to us. Each of us must take off our shoes and meet God on holy ground in our own way.

Seeking Greater Spiritual Resilience and a Healthier Perspective...

- How comfortable are you with solitude with God and "doing nothing" or the space within in order to listen to God? How much do you connect your worth to the work that you do?

DAY 29

> Guilt pushes us to do something good because it is right,
> only love can continually encourage us to do the right thing
> because it is natural.

Guilt certainly has a proper prophetic place in all our lives; it helps to break through the crust of self-righteousness that we all have at some point or other. However, guilt cannot serve as a sustaining force for very long. While guilt pushes us to do something good because it is right, only love can continually encourage us to do the right thing because it is natural.[37]

Given this, the spiritual axiom that seems to be a good summary of the attitude needed in self-examination is: Be clear and be not afraid, for you are loved by God. With this model to guide us, we can seek clarity and do it without fear because, despite our sin, God loves us and has called us friends (John 15:14). So, with this love (based on a deep appreciation of the cross, resurrection, and ministry of Christ), we can, with God's grace, cut through such major enemies of self-awareness as denial, self-reliance, fear of rejection, undue concern with our image or success, and preoccupation with the troubles of the world without a sense of the sovereignty of God.

We also need to recognize how an overreliance on works can lead to undisciplined activism and set us up for spiritual and psychological burnout. This happens when we fail to appreciate the perspective that is an outgrowth of a theology of hope built on faith—and faith in God alone!

Accordingly, with an appreciation of the value of self-awareness and the need for it on the part of the committed person (so that his or her Christian action will remain vital, honest, and prophetic), the following steps are suggested as one way to encourage improved self-awareness:

Take out a pre-established regular time during the day (at noon and in the evening on the way home are often good times) to place yourself in the presence of God for reflection.

Reflect on how you are feeling, thinking, behaving, and imagining yourself (and the world) in light of the call of the gospel to love God, yourself and others.

Pick specific interactions that stand out (negatively/positively) and see what you can learn from them.

Seeking Greater Spiritual Resilience and a Healthier Perspective…

• Which has more power to motivate you, guilt or love? Why might that be the case? What do you need to change?

DAY 30

"We do not see things as they are; we see things as we are."

—THE TALMUD

"If [anyone] loves me, he will keep my word, and my Father will love him and we will come to [them] and make our home with him.... Peace I leave with you; my peace I give to you.... Let not your hearts be troubled, neither let them be afraid."

—JOHN 14:23, 27

Be clear and be not afraid because *you* are loved by God.

Wanting self-knowledge and attaining it are obviously two very radically different things. As Thoreau aptly recognized: "It is as hard to see oneself as to look backwards without turning round."[38] Still, try we must to understand ourselves because, as the Talmudic saying accurately points out: "We do not see things as they are; we see things as we are."

To try to understand ourselves is not easy then. I believe we must have discipline and courage, be specific in our daily reflections, and never forget God's love. Having a practice that encourages good discipline is essential. We must take out time during and at the end of the day to monitor our feelings, thoughts, images, and actions to see what themes arise for us; otherwise, we will just keep moving (maybe in a rut, maybe in the wrong direction—much evil in this world has been done in the name of good!). Taking out even a few minutes for this purpose is not easy though, not only because time is precious, but also because we tend to waste so much of it on action without reflection. When U.S. senator Mark Hatfield was asked what was the greatest challenge facing the senate today, he quickly responded: "Not enough time to think." Today, the same can be said of the church and its committed members.

In line with this, one must have the courage to see with a sense of equanimity our good and bad motivations, our mature and immature agendas and attitudes. Only then can our effort at self-knowledge move with courage to a sense of discovery and hope.

In undertaking self-examination, one must remember to be detailed. Specific interactions need to be monitored so one can avoid hiding behind broad condemnations of others or vague personal repentances. These lead to goals that seldom translate into concrete actions.

And, finally, reflection must be done before a loving God. If it is not, our self-awareness may well become a form of self-condemnation. This, in turn will only lay the foundation for chronic, debilitating guilt or eventual denial instead of spiritual and psychological progress. The simple reason for this is that no one of us likes to look at negative things that we believe will make us feel bad. As a result, behavior we wince at usually turns into behavior that we wink at.[39]

As we try to be present and assist family, friends, and others in need, it is quite easy to lose one's way. Certainly the road to Emmaus can be used as a theme all through one's life of Christian service. We are so blind so much of the time. And much of the blindness we have is traced to losing our way spiritually because we have put our hands around our image, our expectation for dramatic results, or our secret expectations that people will especially love us because we are publicly committed to serve Christ and them. We have forgotten the covenant, forgotten grace…forgotten God. And unfortunately we have forgotten that no matter how talented we are, we must remember Christ's injunction to the apostles: "With [humanity] it is impossible, but not with God: for all things are possible with God" (Mark 10:27).

One of my seminary students quoted the comment of a colleague who taught him an important lesson. He wrote: "When I left seminary I was very capable, and I went out into ministry relying solely on my own gifts and abilities. God rarely came into my equation. Why should God? I seemed to be doing very well on my own. But then after two or three years of 'successful' ministry, I began to realize that there was something missing at the gut level of what I was doing."[40]

We too have been looking for what we may be missing. We have looked at our spirituality—our covenantal relationship with the presence of God. We have sought it in ourselves, others, and in those quiet, solitary, honest encounters with the Lord. We have found it to be essential if we are to continue reaching out to others without being pulled down.

With a deep appreciation of our covenantal spirituality we remember God's love, and we join it with ours so we can live out a passionate ministry with our identity in Christ and continue to say boldly and loudly with the Lord: "I came to cast fire upon the earth; and would that it were already kindled!" (Luke 12:47).

Seeking Greater Spiritual Resilience and a Healthier Perspective...

- What and how have you learned more about yourself during this month? What steps can you take going forward to continue that process?

NOTES

1. Urban Holmes, *Spirituality for Ministry* (San Francisco, Harper and Row, 1982), p. 35.
2. Henri Nouwen, *Clowning in Rome* (New York: Doubleday, 1979), p. 26.
3. Lionel Blue, *Lionel Blue: Selections from His Writings* (Springfield: Templegate, 1987), p. 28.
4. Blue, p. 24.
5. Abraham Heschel, *Quest for God* (New York: Scribners, 1954).
6. James Fenhagen, *Invitation to Holiness* (San Francisco: Harper and Row, 1985), p. 57.
7. "Facing Evil with Maya Angelou," *Moyers & Company,* PBS, August 15, 2014, http://video.pbs.org/video/2365306842/.
8. Karl Rahner, *Words of Faith* (New York: Crossroad, 1987), p. 40.
9. Samuel Dresner, ed., *I Asked for Wonder: A Spiritual Anthology of Abraham Joshua Heschel* (New York: Crossroad, 1986), p. 68.
10. William Glasser, *Reality Therapy* (New York: Harper & Row, 1965).
11. J.P. Dumbois-Dumee, "Renewal of Prayer," *Lumen Vitae,* 38, 3, 1983, pp. 273–274.
12. Basil Pennington, *Thomas Merton, Brother Monk* (San Francisco: Harper & Row, 1987), pp. 24, 25.
13. Pennington, pp. 24, 25.
14. Quoted by Thomas Merton in *A Vow of Conversation,* ed. Naomi Stone Burton (New York: Farrar, Straus, and Giroux, 1988), p. 9.
15. Samuel Dresner, ed., *I Asked for Wonder* (New York: Crossroad, 1986), p. ix.
16. James Finley, *Merton's Palace of Nowhere* (Notre Dame, Ind.: Ave Maria, 1978).
17. Finley.
18. Alice Walker, *The Color Purple* (New York: Harcourt, Brace and Jovanovich, 1982).

19. From an interview with Thich Nhat Hanh in *Common Boundary* (November/December 1989): p. 16.

20. Henri Nouwen, *Making All Things New* (San Francisco: Harper & Row, 1981), p. 33.

21. Maxim Gorky, *Gorky: My Childhood* (London: Penguin, 1966), p. 173.

22. I am grateful to Tommy O'Connor for sharing this experience with me.

23. John Calvin, *Commentaries*, ed. and trans. Joseph Haroutunian and Louise Pettibone Smith, Library of Christian Classics, Vol. 23 (Philadelphia: Westminster, 1958), p. 138. Emphasis added.

24. John Wesley, *The Nature of Spiritual Growth* (Minneapolis: Bethany, 1977), p. 17.

25. John Calvin, *Institutes of the Christian Religion*, ed. J.T. McNeill, The Library of Christian Classics, Vol. 21 (Philadelphia: Westminster, 1960), II, i, p. 1.

26. Calvin, L.i.2. Cf. *Commentary on Isaiah*, 6:5.

27. Robert J. Wicks, *Living Simply in an Anxious World* (Mahwah, N.J.: Paulist, 1988), p. 57.

28. Urban Holmes, *Spirituality for Ministry* (San Francisco: Harper & Row, 1982), p. 150.

29. James Fenhagen, *Invitation to Holiness* (San Francisco: Harper & Row, 1985), p. 57.

30. Quoted in Jack Kornfield, *The Wise Heart: A Guide to the Universal Teaching of Buddhist Psychology* (New York: Bantam, 2009), p. 201.

31. Quoted in Robert Wicks, "Helpful Feedback from Friends," *Catholic Herald*, November 2, 2000, http://catholicherald.com/stories/Helpful-Feedback-from-Friends, 6192.

32. Fred Craddock, *Preaching* (Nashville: Abingdon, 1985), p. 40.

33. Yushi Nomura, *Desert Wisdom: Sayings of the Desert Fathers* (New York: Doubleday, 1982), p. 32.

34. Thomas G. Long, "Why Are We Here," *Testament* 1, no. 1 (November 1989), p. 7.

35. Anthony Bloom, *Beginning to Pray* (Mahwah, N.J.: Paulist, 1970), pp. xv–xvi.

36. Louis A. Vos, "The Christian Self-Image," in *Exploring the Heritage of John Calvin*, ed. David Holwerda (Grand Rapids: Baker, 1976), p. 81.

37. Wicks, *Living Simply in an Anxious World*, p. 40.

38. Henry David Thoreau, quoted by W.H. Auden in his introduction to Dag Hammarskjold's *Markings* (New York: Knopf, 1976), p. ix.

39. Robert J. Wicks, *Availability: The Spritual Joy of Helping Others* (New York: Crossroad, 2000), p.16.

40. Personal correspondence with author.

RECEIVED MAR 2 7 2015

ABOUT THE AUTHOR

Robert J. Wicks received his doctorate in psychology from Hahnemann Medical College and Hospital and is on the faculty of Loyola University, Maryland. He has published more than fifty books for professionals and the general public, including *Bounce: Living the Resilient Life;* *Riding the Dragon;* and *Perspective: The Calm Within the Storm.*